Finding Sane Relationships
in a Crazy World

Cynthia M. Ruiz

BALBOA.
PRESS
A DIVISION OF HAY HOUSE

Balboa Press books may be ordered through booksellers or by contacting:

Balboa Press
A Division of Hay House
1663 Liberty Drive
Bloomington, IN 47403
www.balboapress.com
1-(877) 407-4847

Because of the dynamic nature of the Internet, any web addresses or links contained in this book may have changed since publication and may no longer be valid. The views expressed in this work are solely those of the author and do not necessarily reflect the views of the publisher, and the publisher hereby disclaims any responsibility for them.

ISBN: 978-1-4525-4768-8 (sc)
ISBN: 978-1-4525-4767-1 (e)
Library of Congress Control Number: 2012903503

The author of this book does not dispense medical advice or prescribe the use of any technique as a form of treatment for physical, emotional, or medical problems without the advice of a physician, either directly or indirectly. The intent of the author is only to offer information of a general nature to help you in your quest for emotional and spiritual well-being. In the event you use any of the information in this book for yourself, which is your constitutional right, the author and the publisher assume no responsibility for your actions.

Any people depicted in stock imagery provided by Thinkstock are models, and such images are being used for illustrative purposes only.
Certain stock imagery © Thinkstock.

Printed in the United States of America

Balboa Press rev. date: 2/24/2012

"The story of your life is written by you."

—Don Miguel Ruiz

Acknowledgments

First and foremost, I must acknowledge God. I believe that God is Omnipresent; I believe that God is good and God resides within each of us.

This book is dedicated to two of my exceptional friends who are no longer in this physical world, though they have touched my life and taught me about the value of relationships.

My aunt, Shirley Roberts, has blessed me with her loyalty and wisdom. Though not related by blood, we choose to be family and to be in each other's lives. Our experiences together created many wonderful memories and her courageous spirit lives in my heart.

The second is my beloved friend of twenty-five years, Tad Emery. We spent endless hours talking about life, relationships, and God. Tad's life was an example that miracles do happen. He touched my life in so many ways; I can truly say I have been touched by an angel. He will never be forgotten.

The biggest blessing in my life has been my son, Arturo D. Chavez. Experiencing his unconditional love as a mother has allowed me to experience the joys of happiness and ultimate fulfillment.

As a mother, I am proud of the man he has become. Arturo is intelligent, compassionate, and lives his life with integrity. He has character, is handsome, and can light up a room with his million-dollar smile. Keep smiling.

I also want to give a special thank you to my friend Shawn G. He is the person who gave me the idea for this book because he thought I had a great perspective about relationships. With that suggestion, I meditated; when I woke the next morning, I had the outline for the book. Shawn, you are a very special person, and the differences we both bring to our friendship have made our conversations interesting and thought provoking. I am happy that you have found that sane relationship in your life! I wish you and your family a lifetime of love and happiness.

While on my spiritual journey, I had the good fortune to find the Agape International Spiritual Center (Agape) under the leadership of Reverend Michael Bernard Beckwith. Attending services and classes at Agape has enriched my life. Agape has taught me to say yes to the universe.

As an expression of my gratitude to Agape, a percentage of my proceeds will be donated to the Agape Youth Ministry program. Investing in our youth is a cause that is near and dear to my heart. I believe that it is the responsibility of a leader to turn around and help the next generation.

I send a big hug to Reverend Michael Bernard Beckwith. Your wisdom and teachings have guided me on a path of spiritual empowerment, which has enhanced all areas of my life. The music at Agape has lifted my soul. Rickie Byars Beckwith and the Agage International Choir have allowed my spirit to soar. Once I found Agape, my life was changed forever. I have also committed to donate a percentage of my royalties to the i.am angel foundation. will.i.am is not only a musical genius but is making a positive difference on this planet.

I also want to give a special thank you to all my loving friends I have been blessed to have in my life. There are too many to mention, but you know who you are. I am blessed to have found so many wonderful people to share this journey called life. I have known many of you for over twenty years; you have helped me learn what it takes to develop sustainable relationships and enjoy life to the fullest. I want you to know that I value our time together, our relationships, and our ability to support one another. You add immeasurable value to my life and I hope that I have returned the favor.

People come into your life for a reason, a season, or a lifetime. I am grateful for all my relationships—no matter how long they last. I look forward to many more fun-filled years with the people I have sane relationships with—and I look forward to meeting many more fascinating people along the way.

Thank you, all.

"You can begin to shape your own destiny by the attitude that you keep."
—Michael Bernard Beckwith

Contents

"I've learned that people will forget what you
say, people will forget what you did, but people
will never forget how you made them feel."
—Maya Angelou

Chapter 1:

Relationships in a Crazy World

In today's world, we are surrounded by craziness. All you need to do is turn on the news and you will be bombarded with things that are difficult to comprehend. Thinking about war, social injustice, the world's economic downturn, and global warming is enough to drive anybody crazy.

We live in a time of contradictions:

- There is abundance—yet there is starvation.
- We have money to send people to outer space—yet there is homelessness.
- Technology has connected the world—yet so many people feel alone.
- Our society is obsessed with youth—yet we are living longer and the number of seniors is increasing.

In recent times, we have seen many people act out in horrific ways and resort to killing others. Multiple shootings have become far too common, especially from our youth.

Many times, people act irrationally just to get attention. At an early age, some people learn that negative actions can get attention.

Some hold the viewpoint that negative attention is better than no attention at all.

We have more stress in our lives than ever! It can be challenging to find constructive ways of dealing with all the stressors of modern life:

- We can feel stress at work and while fighting traffic in our daily commute.
- Pressure to be an ideal parent, spouse, or friend can make us anxious.
- We compete to go to the top school, get the best job, make the most money, and purchase the largest house.
- We strive for perfection when it comes to our appearance, to being beautiful or handsome, to looking young, and to being skinny.

This stress and craziness makes it that much more important to find healthy relationships that support us and shower us with unconditional love.

Sane relationships can be your sanctuary, providing you with serenity and security. Unconditional love can restore your balance, which nurtures our inner peace. I know we have all felt out of balance at one time or another. That sensation of feeling out of sorts makes us less productive, unhappy, and insecure.

We know that having even one bad relationship can consume one's time and energy. There are some relationships that thrive on drama and can knock one out of balance very easily if the drama is persistent. The key to a fulfilling life is to find balance and harmony in all areas of your life. A good place to start is by creating sane relationships around you.

I strive to have healthy relationships at my work, in my personal life, and in daily encounters with people. I also choose to eliminate chronic toxic relationships so I may experience a sense of personal freedom and happiness.

This book is meant to help you with your relationships—and to assist you in becoming a satisfied person. I humbly share with you the lessons I have learned as I have moved along my path of spiritual awakening and personal freedom. I do not claim to have all of the answers. I simply ask that you keep an open mind.

This book follows a simple workbook format so you can have the tools necessary to do the work to get to a place where you can experience satisfying relationships. As with most things in life, if you make the effort, you will enjoy the results.

I have also included some of my favorite quotes from people who have inspired me. There are many great teachers with great ideas. We can all learn from each other.

The point of finding sane relationships is to enjoy other people. If I can touch your life in a positive way or inspire you toward a path of having healthy relationships, then I have accomplished what I have set out to do. For some, it will resonate more than others because we are all at different points in our lives. Life is a journey—not a destination.

So enjoy your journey, be open to receiving new lessons, and find relationships that work for you! I believe it is not the number of relationships in your life—it is the quality of those relationships.

I often say, "I love my life and I am grateful." I am grateful for the, people in my life and, the opportunities to learn and grow each and every day I choose to see the blessings in my life and I look forward to the blessings yet to come.

It is not that I have a perfect life. I certainly have had my share of trials and tribulations. I am not even clear about what a perfect life is supposed to be. I am not living in denial about the challenges that appear in my life. Just living on this planet will bring challenges to anyone, but how we choose to move through those challenges will allow you to see them as blessings or not. Having sane relationships will make getting through the challenges a bit easier. I have a strong support network and try to maintain positive relationships. I know that I can overcome whatever stumbling blocks life puts in front of me.

There is no perfect life, but when you learn how to master your reactions to life's challenges and surround yourself with sane people, your life will become perfect for you. I hope that you love your life!

Relationships

A general definition of the word relationship is "dealing or associations." It also defines a relationship as a significant connection or similarity between two or more things, or the state of being related to something else.

We interact with many people throughout our lives. During our social development years, we interact with parents, siblings, teachers, friends, and extended family members. However, interfacing with people around you does not necessarily mean that you have a healthy relationship with them.

As we grow into adulthood, we learn that not all relationships are healthy—and not all relationships are created equal. If we are fortunate, we realize that we have choices when it comes to relationships. If we find ourselves in relationships that become abusive, negative, or unhealthy, we know we have the option of letting it go. Once you understand that you have a choice in relationships, it becomes easier to let go of the nonproductive relationships in your life.

Some people focus on changing the other person—or the way they act—in order to make the relationship better. We cannot change other people, but we can change how we relate to or interact with the other person. We have control only over our side of the relationship and our actions. We have a choice over whether or not we participate in a particular situation.

The key to a gratifying life is to find balance. Why should relationships be any different? I strive to have healthy relationships with the people I care about and eliminate the toxic relationships. As a result, I have experienced a sense of personal freedom.

When most of us think of past events and savor memories, they usually involve others. Our successes and failures are usually shared with the people in our life. Healthy and sane relationships can bring great joy to your life. Having people to share the positive events and the challenges in your life can be some of the biggest rewards in life.

Since you are reading this book, you must be interested in developing some healthy relationships in your life. You may want to improve some relationships and shed others. A few bad relationships may pop into your mind that you are not sure what to do with.

Well, you have taken the first step by picking up this book. You may be interested in improving your relationships or finding new ones that meet your needs. Positive relationships can enrich your life with harmony and fulfillment.

Humans are social creatures by nature. Social interaction is a part of what helps us develop a sense of relationship to the world around us. It gives us perspective. It helps celebrate the good times, and it provides us with a safety net when we fall. Without a safety net, some plunge into a place of darkness and despair.

In 1943, American psychologist Abraham Maslow developed the "hierarchy of needs." Maslow believed that after physiological and safety needs are fulfilled, the third layer of human needs are social and involve feelings of belongingness. This aspect of Maslow's hierarchy involves emotionally based relationships:

- friendship
- intimacy
- family

Humans need to feel a sense of belonging and acceptance. Whether it comes from a large social group (clubs, office culture, religious groups, professional organizations, sports teams, gangs) or small social connections (family members, intimate partners, mentors, colleagues, or confidants), they need to love and be loved (sexually and non-sexually) by others.

In the absence of these elements, many people become susceptible to loneliness, social anxiety, and clinical depression. Without the benefit of positive relationships, some people end up in a deep depression, have no sense of belonging, or feel alone. The extreme of this is hopelessness; people without hope cannot see a future.

Therefore, this book will assist you in developing your skills to mastering sane relationships. It will help you achieve a sense of support and belonging. However, to reap the benefits of this book, you need to be brutality honest with yourself. Honesty is the only way that this will work for you. It will enhance your happiness.

I recommend starting with an inventory of who is currently in your life. This will serve as a baseline. What relationships (good or bad) are you participating in?

Find some quiet time where you will not have interruptions or distractions. Unplug the phone, turn off your cell phone, Blackberry, or iPhone and get started. This may feel awkward—but consider it as an investment in you. No one lives in a vacuum; we are connected to each other.

Relationship Inventory (RI), Who is in your life?

Take out a pen and paper (you may also choose to do this on a computer, which is just as effective). If you are the type of person that does not like to make lists, make a mental note. Do what feels right.

- Take a moment to list the people in your life.
- Think about them individually. Say their name a few times either quietly or out loud. Note the first thing that comes to your mind. It can be an adjective, feeling, or emotion.

Observe how you feel when you think about that person and make some notes. Honesty is very important. You do not have to show the list to anyone. This is for your growth and you get to decide if you want to share it with others.

• Repeat this exercise for each person on the list with a brief pause in between.

Relationship Inventory
(Sample)

Name	Thoughts	Feelings
Bill	Strong and compassionate. I think he will always be there for me.	I feel love toward him.
Mary	Drama, likes to gossip. She is self-centered and has a big ego.	I feel like I can't trust her.
Jim	Makes me laugh, fun. He is always interesting and intriguing.	I feel happy when he is around.
Sue	Smart, loving, enjoys life.	I feel loved and cared for by her.
John	Always depressed and negative. Always plays the victim.	I feel uneasy around him.
Eric	Friend for many years. I can always count on him to be there.	I feel unconditional love.
Anne	Loves life, outgoing, positive, and a true friend.	I feel a deep connection to her.

Depending on the number of people in your life, you may not get through the entire list in one sitting. It is all right to put it aside and come back to the list at a later date.

It is also good to give yourself some space before you revisit your inventory. Once you have created your inventory, go back and look at *your* participation in each relationship:

- What do you do to keep this relationship healthy?
- Do you provide unconditional love and support?
- How do you add value and joy to the other person's life?
- Are you judgmental and critical?
- Are you honest and sincere?
- Are you a good listener?
- Are you involved with that person out of habit?

If you feel any negativity when you think of a certain person, examine it. What is the origin of those feelings?

Relationships can be affected by unresolved feelings. One person may be holding anger, resentment, guilt, or other emotions. These unresolved emotions and feelings might be having an impact on the current situation.

Update Your Relationship Inventory on an Annual Basis

You may wish to revisit this relationship inventory from time to time. Since relationships change with time and experience, it is important to keep a regular check-in as your life evolves.

The fascinating thing about relationships is that they are dynamic and evolve as people change. No two relationships are exactly the same. No two people are exactly alike. We all bring our experience and perceptions into each relationship (good or bad).

You can also reevaluate your inventory after you finish this book because your perspective may change, which can influence your participation in relationships.

Now that you have completed your inventory, let's move on to believing that you should have sane relationships in your life.

After you have established who is in your life, you have to believe that you deserve sane relationships. A good technique is using positive affirmations. They help reprogram the brain. They will teach you to incorporate new ways of thinking into your daily life. Repetition works in positive affirmations.

A positive affirmation programs these positive thoughts and beliefs into my mind. You can say them out loud or write them down:

- I deserve sane relationships in my life.
- I want healthy relationships in my life.
- I am manifesting more love in my life than I can even imagine.
- I love being loved.
- I love giving love.

If you are saying them out loud, repeat them louder. Say them like you really mean them—from the depths of your soul.

- I deserve sane relationships in my life.
- I want healthy relationships in my life.
- I am manifesting more love in my life than I can even imagine.
- I love being loved.
- I love giving love.

If none of these sentences resonates with you, feel free to make up your own affirmations in a way that feels comfortable for you. You need to say words that have meaning to you.

I _____ relationships in my life.

Write them down and post them in places where you will see them daily. Post on the mirror, in your car, your computer, or wherever you will see them on a regular basis. We all need reminders so we can reprogram old thought patterns.

If you do not feel comfortable posting them, use the notes section on your Blackberry, iPad, or iPhone. Everyone needs to find out what works for him or her.

Triggers are reminders that help you remember to review the affirmations. It can be a picture, an object, or something else that will trigger your thoughts to remember to say these affirmations.

You have now finished the first step toward finding sane relationships by establishing an inventory, demonstrating a willingness to participate in healthy relationships, and accepting that you deserve constructive relationships. You are off to a great start!

Change and Dynamic Relationships

Relationships are evolving processes. A good relationship can turn into a bad relationship for many reasons and vice versa.

I realize that I am not the same person I was ten years ago—or even five years ago. I work at evolving as a person. These changes have influenced some of my relationships.

People change, outside influences affect people, people grow, and sometimes we grow apart. Drugs and alcohol can change a person's behavior. The one thing that you can be sure about in this world is change. Like it or not, there is going to be change. By human nature, we don't like change; however, the more you adapt to change, the happier you will become.

People may react differently to trauma. Some people internalize it, but others take it out on the people they are closest to or people they don't know.

An extreme example of this is road rage. Some people take their anger out on other drivers. It has gotten to the point where some drivers shoot other drivers. How crazy is that?

If someone accidently cuts you off on the freeway, is it really worth shooting him or her? Well, of course not. To me, it shows that the shooter has reached a point of unhappiness and wants to hurt others. Their pain and anger is demonstrated in lashing out at others. Unless you address these underlying negative feelings they will have an impact on your relationships with other people.

"We can never obtain peace in the outer
world until we make peace within ourselves."
—Dalai Lama

"Building this day on a foundation of pleasant thoughts. Never fret at any imperfections that you fear may impede your progress. Remind yourself, as often as necessary, that you are a creature of God and have the power to achieve any dream by lifting up your thoughts. You can fly when you decide that you can. Never consider yourself defeated again. Let the vision in your heart be in your life's blueprint. Smile!"

—Og Mandino

Chapter 2:

Foundation for Sane Relationships

Many people fail to understand that relationships need a solid foundation to hold them together through thick and thin. A house without a secure foundation could fall apart when impacted by environmental elements. Without a solid foundation, you have nothing to build on.

You are the foundation on which all relationships in your life are built. You need that foundation so the relationships in your life can be healthy and balanced.

Now that you have established the relationships in your life, you need to identify the principles that are essential in a good relationship. A healthy relationship should be built on the following:

- communication
- honesty
- trust
- respect
- reciprocity

You can also identify what you feel are the pillars of a healthy relationship. I am sharing what works for me.

Communication

Communication is the cornerstone of all relationships. It sounds easy, right? If it is, why are there so many miscommunications? Seek clarification if you are not sure what someone else is trying to communicate. Do not assume if you are not sure.

In situations when I thought I understood what another person was trying to communicate to me, I have been wrong. My perception was based on my reality, but the communication was based on his perception of reality. Everyone's reality is different and perception is different for different people. With communication, we are forced to rely on words. Language can be influenced by culture. Words have different meanings and different meanings to different people.

Did you ever play the game of telephone when you were a kid? The first person shares a statement with the next person; by the time it goes around the group, it turns out to be something completing different. We all laugh and say how crazy it is that we ended up with something that was so different from where we started. It is a combination of miscommunications and differences in the way we perceive things based on our individual reality. That is why it is so important in relationships to have clear communication.

Clarify things if you are not sure. Ask the other person to repeat what they said if you are not sure. Be clear about the other person's intended meaning. It is also very important to choose your words wisely. Mean what you say and say what you mean. The other person is not a mind reader.

Young children are good at speaking without a filter. They say exactly what is on their minds. Sometimes they are so brutally honest that it can be funny. As we become adults, we learn to use filters. Filters are used so you do not hurt other people feelings or appear rude. Filters are usually influenced by society and what is acceptable behavior. Some people allow their words to be influenced by what they think others want to hear. Don't allow your opinions to be compromised just to make others happy.

As you live your life and have new experiences, your thoughts and perceptions can change. Your past experiences become your point of reference. Emotions can also impact communication. What you said when you were angry may not be what you really meant. Most of us have experienced saying something in anger and wishing we could retract it. However, once it is out there, it is too late. It is more productive to have important conversations when we are not angry or frustrated. Allow yourself to cool down before having that important conversation.

Honesty

The truth will set you free. Sometimes when you meet someone new, human nature is to put our best foot forward. We tend not to be completely honest because we do not want to feel vulnerable. Insecurities tend to arise and we question our self-worth. We think that the person may not like us if they really know us. Sometimes people fail to tell the entire truth—or they exaggerate. If you are not honest, your relationship will not have a solid foundation.

When you find out that someone is not honest with you, what is the first thing you think? *If this person has lied to me about this, what else have they lied about?*

Without honesty how can there be trust? *If this person lies to me, how can I trust them to tell the truth in the future?*

Trust

English author Ann Radcliffe said, "I never trust people's assertions, I always judge of them by their actions."

According to the Merriam Webster dictionary, trust is defined as reliance on the integrity, strength, ability, surety of a person or thing; confidence, or confident expectation of something.

Sometimes trust is given in a relationship but is taken away as actions produce results. Other times, it is earned over time. What does trust mean in a relationship?

Ask yourself these questions:

- Do you trust that the other person is not going to hurt you?
- Do you trust that they are going to be loyal?
- Do you trust that they will tell you the truth?
- Do you trust that they will be there for you in your time of need?

In my opinion, it is all of above and more. For me, trust takes time and is not automatic. I evaluate whether or not the words match the actions. If I hear one thing but see a different action, it will be difficult for me to trust.

Remember that trust is a two-way street. If your actions do not match your words, the other person may not trust you.

Respect

Respect is to hold in esteem or honor or to show regard or consideration. It is something that we all want. No one likes to feel disrespected. When you feel disrespected, you feel as if the other person does not value your feelings. Being disrespected can lead to resentment or grudges that can turn to anger. If you feel disrespected in some of your relationships, discuss it and resolve it as soon as possible. If you cannot resolve it then you do have a choice about continuing the relationship.

Reciprocity

Another key component of a relationship is reciprocity. If neither person is benefiting from the relationship, it is not healthy. Some people only take—and never give anything—emotionally, physically, mentally, or spiritually.

You may want to ask yourself if this person will be there if you need something. If you find no benefit in the relationship, it may be time to release them. Life is never completely balanced. In long-term relationships, there is often a seesaw effect. One person may give more for a while—and the other may reciprocate later—but it should even out.

You need to find the delicate balance that accommodates both people's needs. On the other hand, you need to take a look in the mirror to make sure you are not the one doing all the taking. If it does apply to you, you have the power to change.

If you find additional characteristics that you want to include in the qualities you are looking for in relationships, add as many as necessary to assist you in identifying qualities that are important to you.

"Insist on yourself. Never imitate."
—Ralph Waldo Emerson

"Though you may travel the world to
find the beautiful, you must have it
within you or you will find it not."

—Ralph Waldo Emerson

Chapter 3:

Self-Love and Happiness:
It Starts with Me

Before you can participate in a healthy relationship with another person, you need to have a healthy relationship with yourself. You already know that you are the foundation of all your relationships. When most people hear self-love, they think it is saying, "I love myself." However, in order to have self-love, your thoughts and actions have to be in alignment.

Most people say, "Of course I love myself. Who doesn't?" In reality, many of us don't—and we may not even realize it. On the surface you might, but your actions can be telling a different story. Pay attention to your behavior.

Having a strong sense of worth and self-esteem are critical components of self-love. It is vital to be happy in your own skin and enjoy who you are. The beauty of life is that we are all different—no two people are alike. It is important to be happy with yourself and not want to be someone else. If you do not love yourself, how can you expect anyone else to love you? That is not to say you won't have relationships—they just won't necessarily be healthy ones full of love and joy.

Many people base happiness and self-love on material things:

- If I have more money, I will be happy.
- If I have a bigger house, I will be happy.
- If I have a good-looking spouse, I will be happy.
- If I get that diamond ring, I will be happy.

Whatever the case, many people look toward external factors for fulfillment. It is easy to get caught up in the race to have the best to be happy. The United States is a consumer-driven society, but do those material things really make you happy? Of course not. However, advertisers try to sell us on these ideas so they can sell more cars, clothes, or products.

There are plenty of examples of wealth not bringing happiness. Take a few minutes to think about what makes you happy. Use this opportunity to list things that are not material in nature. For example, I enjoy spending time with my son, hiking, socializing with my friends, going to concerts, and walking my dogs. I have found that the simple things in life bring me the greatest joy.

Self-Love

Self-love should not be confused with narcissism. The negative extreme of self-love happens when a person is out of balance and is extremely self-centered. They only think of themselves and do not do well in relationships. I think we have all encountered people like this at one time or another.

So let's evaluate your self-love.

- Do you like you?

Be sincere and ask yourself the following questions:

Are you afraid to be alone?

There is a difference between being alone and being lonely. If you love yourself, you should feel good when you are alone. As a matter of fact, you might really like your alone time. Having some alone time is part of having a balanced life.

Can you spend time by yourself and be okay?

Do you feel fear, anxiety, or a general uneasiness when alone? As soon as you are alone, do you wish you had someone with you? Do you think you could only be happy if you had your spouse, girlfriend or boyfriend, family, or friends with you? Do you feel bored when no one else is around?

Do you not feel incomplete unless you are in the company of another?

Some of us rely on other people to make us happy.

- I am not happy, and it is my spouse's fault.
- I am not happy, and it is my boss's fault, my mom's fault, etc.
- He or she no longer makes me happy.

Is it really someone else's responsibility to make us happy? No, we are—and should be—responsible for *our own* happiness.

When you care about someone, it is normal to feel happy when you see or spend time with him or her. However, it is not their job to make you feel happy. You need to take ownership of your happiness.

Happiness is subjective. What makes one person happy may not make you happy. Take a look at what makes you happy. Try to evaluate your social network, work, family, and friends with a holistic perspective.

"Happiness depends upon ourselves."
—Aristotle

Self-Happiness Evaluation (SHE Test).

Take a minute in a quiet place and ask yourself the follow question what percentage of the time you are happy and what percentage of the time you are not happy. Be honest because if you cannot be honest with yourself, you are probably not honest with others. Making the needed changes in your life requires that you be open and honest.

What percentage of the time am I happy?
... And what percentage of the time am I not happy?

You should answer this question as an average over a period of time. You can choose to look at the last five years, five months, or five weeks. Pick a time frame that works for you.

If you are having trouble, you can keep it simple and look at today. Am I happy today? Understand that every day is different—and we all have good days and bad days. Most people never ask themselves this type of question. We go through life without evaluating it—or our happiness.

Nobody is cheerful all of the time—life just does not work like that. I am happy 95 percent of the time. I have worked to clear out things in my life to get there—and it has been worth the effort. Since everyone is different, try not to compare yourself to anyone else. However, the closer you are to 100 percent, the better your life will be.

Since I am a visual person, it was helpful to put it in a format that I can see. I entered my results on a pie chart. You can do that for your results. It is always good to see a visual of your life. We have thoughts but once you see it in black and white you get a better understanding of the concept.

Once you have determined what percent of the time you are happy, give yourself a grade based on the table below:

A	90 to 100
B	80 to 89
C	70 to 79
D	60 to 69
F	Below 59

Be as honest as possible when doing this evaluation—you only hurt yourself if you are not willing to look in the mirror. The results of this exercise will be a tool in determining whether you are ready for sane relationships.

So what does your score mean?

First take a look at the time frame you used. If you used the last six months as your gauge, then let's take a look at that. If you said you are happy 75 percent % of the time, then that means you are unhappy 25 percent % of the time. 25 percent % of six months is 1.5 months, which equals 45 days or 1,080 hours. Why would anyone want to walk around unhappy for 1,080 hours? Life is too short.

A: You are happy most of the time and are on the right path. You are balanced and probably have a positive attitude. You realize that you control your own destiny. You can handle the challenges that life puts in your path.

B: You are happy the vast majority of the time. You are doing well but have room for improvement. Take a look at the areas in your life where you can change. You almost there just need a few minor adjustments in your life.

C: Not being happy 30 percent of the time translates to 216 hours per month. That equals nine days in one month that you are not happy. It is time to take up some hobbies and find your passion.

It is also time to reevaluate the inventory of the relationships in your life and maybe do some housecleaning. You have the power to change your life.

D: If you are not feeling satisfied or fulfilled 40 percent of the time, take time to find your passion. Take a deep look at what is preventing you from being happy and work on letting go of your issues. Reevaluate the inventory of the relationships in your life and do some housecleaning. The weight of the past is holding you back from your happiness.

If you are happy less than 59 percent of the time, now is the time to work on yourself and start enjoying life. This does not mean doomsday—it just means you really need to turn your thoughts around and enjoy life. Your life is made up of your thoughts. Start focusing on the positive not the negative. Focus on what you have not what you do not have. In the morning, create a gratitude list. Be grateful for the small things in your life. If you are not happy, why would anyone want to be around you?

The good news is that once you work on your issues, you can increase your happiness. Increased happiness gives rise to joy and attracts people to you. Your degree of happiness is something you have the power to change. It takes a conscious effort, but you will see tangible results if you do the work.

You may want to come back to this exercise in a few months if things have changed for you. Once you learn that you are responsible for your happiness, you can control the outcome.

So what stops us from loving our self and being happy?

When we were young, we were happy and capable of loving others and ourselves. So what changed? Over the years, we had various experiences that caused different emotions.

Here are some examples of emotions that can impede our self-love and happiness:

- guilt
- buried secrets
- insecurities
- fear
- being a victim

Guilt

Guilt can be created by something that you have done or something that was done to you. Everyone makes mistakes, but the key to being happy is learning from the mistake, releasing the guilt associated with the mistake, and moving on. Learning from the experience is essential for releasing the guilt.

No one is perfect—it not productive to beat yourself up when the past cannot be changed. Do not live in the past. It is hard to feel guilty about the future or something that has not yet happened so do not worry about the future. Let go of the guilt that is causing your unhappiness.

You need to work through any issues you have associated with guilt and let go of them so they don't interfere with your current relationships. Later in the book you will learn some tools on how to let go.

Buried Secrets

Buried secrets create issues in our lives that don't allow us to be in integrity with who we are. These can be feelings of shame, guilt, or anger. If we are not in integrity with ourselves, it will be difficult to have a sane relationship.

Releasing a buried secret can bring people together or reveal the people who are supposed to be in our lives. As we experience unpleasant events in our life, one of our defense mechanisms we use is to bury the memory of the event. We do not want to think about it because there is pain associated with memory. It can be something horrific such as being abused as a child. We suppress the memory because of the pain but sooner or later it will surface and can come out in unexpected way. Facing it head on is not easy but will help with relationships.

Forgiveness is a powerful tool.

Forgiveness plays a big role in resolving buried secrets. Forgiveness can be forgiving others or self-forgiveness. Unconditional love is often derived when a secret is being revealed and or released through forgiveness.

Insecurities

Most people have some type of insecurity—and it can block us from happiness. Insecurities are individual and usually based on what we perceive to be lacking within or what we have been told is lacking. Insecurities can range from feeling too fat, skinny, tall, short, old, young, educated, uneducated, etc.

Somehow we feel different from the norm. Insecurities are common; it really comes down to a matter of degree. However, if the insecurity is so great that it stops us from loving ourselves, then it can lead to self-destructive behaviors. People develop eating disorders or become addicted to drugs, alcohol, sex, food, shopping, or gambling. Self-abuse of any kind is not good.

Feeling that we are missing out on something or lacking something in our lives may cause unhappiness:

- If I had a fancy car, I would be happy.
- If I had a big house, I would be happy.
- If I was famous, I would be happy.
- If I had a lot of money, I would be happy.

Feeling as if we lack something causes insecurity. It is important to realize that you have everything you need—if you look within. You do not need material things or money to make you happy.

Fear

Fear can be a strong emotion that gets in the way of living a full life. It could be fear of being alone, fear of commitment, or fear of getting hurt. Everyone has experienced fear. A phobia is an intense and persistent fear of certain situations, activities, things, animals, or people.

Fear is normal in certain situations. In a robbery, you most likely experience fear. However, if fear is affecting your relationships, you need to take a look at the cause. Losing a parent at a young age can develop into a fear of abandonment that can manifest in different ways. The person may not let anyone in his or her life or become needy and clingy.

Fear that has not been dealt with can turn into anxiety. Anxiety can eventually have physical consequences. These unresolved emotions can have a negative impact on relationships.

Victim Role

Playing the victim role is un-empowering. Some of the many examples are as follows:

- I am not happy, because no one likes me.
- I am not happy, because I do not have enough money.
- I am not happy, because I am not skinny enough.
- I am not happy, because something happened when I was a child.
- I am not happy, because no one will help me.

The list has endless possibilities for statement of being a victim. If you allow yourself to stay in the victim role, you will never be truly happy because you have given your power to someone or something else to decide your state of being. It will always be someone else's fault. You will never take responsibility for your own happiness.

Taking responsibility for your thoughts and actions will empower you! If you love yourself, others will follow. If you do not like yourself, why should others?

"The love that you withhold is
the pain that you carry."
—Ralph Waldo Emerson

"Hatred paralyzes life: love releases it.
Hatred confuses life: love harmonizes it.
Hatred darkens life; love illuminates it."

—Martin Luther King Jr.

Chapter 4:

Release & Let Go of What Holds You Back from Your Happiness.

We can change our level of happiness if we release our outstanding issues and realize we are whole and complete as we are. We do not lack anything—all of our needs are met. It is our perception versus our acceptance of where we are in our lives that holds us back.

Don't fall into the trap of comparing yourself to others to measure your success or happiness. I am not happy because my neighbor has a new boat and I don't. My older brother is better than I am because he has a better paying job. We each have our own life to live. No two people have the exact same experiences—and everyone has their own journey. Why would we compare ourselves to anyone else?

People also have different ways of reacting to experiences. Siblings can react differently to the same traumatic experience. One may come through the situation a stronger person while the other may be traumatized by the experience.

A common example would be a family going through a divorce. One child may be relieved by the divorce because the parents were no longer fighting. Another child may allow it to affect future relationships by developing a fear of commitment. *If I don't get married, I will never have to feel the pain of divorce.*

The next biggest stumbling block to our happiness is holding on to something from our past. This could be a memory of a specific situation, event, or condition. The memory of this event holds us back because the event usually happened many years earlier. Its memory blocks us from living in the present moment.

Let's work through the issues that block us from complete happiness. The obstacles can be removed and you can be free to enjoy today.

Release and Letting Go Exercise (RLGE)

Find a block of time when you will not be interrupted. You will need a pen and paper or your computer. Turn off your cell phone and let others know you need some alone time. Allow yourself a few hours if you are serious about doing the work.

This exercise can be difficult or painful. It may stir up unresolved emotions or difficult memories. Many of us have buried these unpleasant memories for self-protection. You may even need to cry. That is normal—even for men. Some of this may have been with you for years. Everyone carries around baggage. Let go of that baggage—it is too cumbersome to carry that weight on your shoulders.

Close your eyes, and let your mind wonder. Sit still for a few minutes and take a few deep breathes. Breathe in and breathe out. With your eyes still closed think about your life. Start with your childhood and work your way to the present. If any of the memories are unpleasant, evaluate what feelings are associated with the memories.

Start by identifying the memories or thoughts that are stopping you from being happy. Write them down. There may be a few items on the list—or a lot. If there is a lot of unhappiness in your life, the list may be long.

What have you been carrying around?

- Maybe you never felt good enough because your father always liked your older brother better than he liked you.
- Your high school teacher said you would never amount to anything.
- The kids in the schoolyard made fun of you because you were too fat or too skinny.
- You took money from your neighbor when you were a kid.
- Your ex cheated on you.
- Your were abused as a child.
- You did something you are ashamed of.

After you have identified the obstacles to your happiness—events, thoughts, or memories—it is time to release them.

Take your list, read each one aloud, and say, "I release this and will no longer allow this to stand in the way of my happiness. I deserve to be happy."

For example:

- "I release the memory of not being good enough when I was fourteen. I release this and will no longer allow this to stand in the way of my happiness. I deserve to be happy."
- "I release the time my mother told me I was not her favorite child. I release this, and I will no longer allow it to stand in the way of my happiness. I deserve to be happy."

You can repeat this as many times as you need to. You may cry while doing the release work. A good cry helps you release the emotions that surround the memory.

Once you have gone through each item, release the entire list in a symbolic gesture of letting the memory go:

- Throw the list away.
- Cut up the list with scissors.
- Shred the list with a paper shredder.
- Burn the list (my favorite).

I like to burn it with a white candle because I can literally see it go up in smoke. I use a white candle to represent purity. You can even throw it into your fireplace if you have one.

If you that have a lot of release work to do, write each thought or memory on a separate sheet of paper and release one at a time. You may not get to all of them in one sitting. Do what works best for you!

About a month after completing your release work, go back and retake the SHE test. If you have truly released your obstacles, your percentage of happiness should have increased.

If your percentage has not gone up, you need to repeat the release work as many times as it takes to let go of the past.

Release work can be rewarding, but it can also be a little awkward if you have never done it before. If you have been carrying the baggage around for many years, it may not be easy to let it go. Be patient with yourself and keep doing the work. Once you do the release work, you may feel a sense of freedom and satisfaction. Others may feel confused or uneasy once the emotions surface. Those unsettling feelings will not last.

Why is release work so important? It helps us live in the moment. We enjoy relationships in the moment. It helps us enjoy what is in front of us today. So many people live in the past or in the future. To truly savor your healthy relationships, you will need to enjoy the moment.

You will be a more fulfilled person once you realize what you have control over and what is not within your control. This may be a good time to use some version of the serenity prayer.

> "God grant me the serenity
> to accept the things I cannot change;
> courage to change the things I can;

and wisdom to know the difference."

Once you release the old thought patterns, you will be ready to participate in healthier, more productive relationships.

"It takes a lot of courage to release the familiar and seemingly secure, to embrace the new. But there is no real security in what is no longer meaningful. There is more security in the adventurous and exciting, for in movement there is life, and in change there is power."

—Alan Cohen

"Life is the flower of which love is the honey."
—Jean Baptiste Alphonse Karr

Chapter 5:

Relationships with Significant Others

We all have feminine and masculine energy. Carl Jung called it the yin and the yang. Finding that balance of the two takes work. Keeping that balance can be influenced by our relationships.

When we use the term relationship, most people think of a relationship with a significant other (boyfriend, girlfriend, husband, wife, or life partner). Adults have many types of relationships, but our relationship with a significant other can be one of the most influential. This stems from a deep desire to love and be loved.

Over the past few decades, the changing roles of the sexes have had an impact on the dynamics of relationships. Some people say that things were simpler when the male was the provider and the woman was the homemaker. The roles were clearly defined. Relationships lasted longer because everyone knew what was expected of them. Of course, there was also an expectation to stay with a spouse no matter what was happening in the relationship.

For some, divorce was not an option because of societal expectations or religious beliefs. Some couples stayed together whether they were happy or not.

Today's relationships are complicated because the world is complicated. Roles are changing, expectations are changing, and the stress of making a living affects our lives in a more intense manner.

Divorce is at an all-time high. It is not uncommon for people in their forties or fifties to be on a second marriage—or a third. This presents a new set of challenges, including ex-husbands, ex-wives, stepchildren, etc. The model of the blended family—yours, mine, and ours—is becoming a common occurrence.

Even the dating arena seems to have changed. Most people tend to hang out in groups rather that the old fashioned way of dating. Many people are using the Internet as a dating tool. Speed dating has become a trend and there is less one-on-one personal interaction.

So how do you really get to know someone? The answer is simple: time. It really takes time to get to know another person. Most people are still scratching the surface after dating for six months.

People are eager to jump into a relationship for various reasons. Insecurity is one. The need to be with someone because they are afraid of being alone is one of the biggest reasons. Your expectations and perceptions about someone are based on your past perceptions and beliefs and may not reflect the person at all. We all have in our mind what our ideal person should be like. This can be shaped by society, family, friends, or the media.

Some women are looking for their knight in shining armor or Prince Charming. These characters carry a woman off into the sunset to live happily ever after. Unfortunately, when this expectation is applied to a real-life relationship—and the man does not live up to this expectation—disappointment ensues.

Men often have a different perception of a woman for their relationships. They are much more visual and have an idea of a woman who is going to look like a *Playboy* Playmate. They idealize the sex goddess and look for physical beauty. If they only knew how many people it takes to make those pictures look perfect, their reality may be altered. For that one glamour shot to be used in a magazine, the team includes make-up artists, hair stylists, wardrobe stylists, photographers, lighting technicians, and graphic artists to enhance the photo in Photoshop. These examples are not realistic for most people.

Sometimes our expectations are not even realistic. Many women are raised to find Mr. Right and get married. When we don't find him (mostly since Mr. Right does not exist), we try to change the person to meet our perception of Mr. Right.

Another way that expectations can influence relationships is the idea that you can change the other person. For example, women may get together with a man who is known for being a womanizer. She begins the relationship with the expectation that she can change him, but you cannot turn an alley cat into a house cat.

Men try to change women in different ways. If a man begins a relationship with a woman who dressed to accentuate her assets, then as soon as he is in a relationship with her, he wants her to dress in a way that makes her unattractive. Is that realistic? This could result in arguments or unhealthy dynamics. It is important to take the time to get to know the other person before you commit or get married.

Before you start a relationship, ask yourself what you want in a person. Make a list of the things that are important in a mate and describe what type of relationship you want. You may want someone who is humorous, intelligent, confident, or kind. Prioritize and identify where you are willing to compromise if needed, but know your deal breakers!

- Children: Don't assume that all men or women want children. More women are deciding that they want to focus on their careers and that they do not want children. Maybe they already have children. Some people feel it is too much responsibility to be involved with someone who already has children. Raising another person's children is a big commitment.

- Religion: For some people, it is a priority to find someone with the same religious beliefs.
- Educational level is important to some.
- Height, weight, or other physical attributes are important to some.
- Political affiliations are important to some.

Decide what is a deal breaker in your particular situation and set of circumstances. Be honest with yourself about what is important to you.

Know what type of relationship you are looking for because everyone has different needs and desires. Are you looking to start a family? Are you interested in marriage, companionship, sexual satisfaction, casual dating, or just friendship? Some desire financial security or emotional support. Know what you want.

- Close your eyes and visualize the person.
- Feel the energy of that person.
- Set the intention for that special someone to come into your life.
- Expect that you will get everything you want and/or better.

When the special person comes into your life—and you have open communication—talk about what is important to you.

- Do you have common goals?
- Is there enough common ground for the relationship to be sustainable?
- Do both people want the same thing out of the relationship?
- Do you communicate effectively?
- Do you set boundaries?
- Do you come together with through a difficult experience open to growth and change?

Even if you are in a relationship, it is still a good idea to make a list of what type of person you want in a relationship. It is an individual decision whether to share the list with your significant other. If they are not a close match, you may not want to make them feel insecure or uncomfortable. However, it may be time to reevaluate the relationship or discuss potential growth opportunities with your partner.

We also need to remember that people change and evolve; we are very different in our twenties than in our forties or sixties. We go through different stages in our lives and have different experiences that shape who we are.

Once we find someone, it is important to have a solid foundation and commitment to keep growing as a couple. Just as we have different stages in our lives, we can have different stages in our relationships. When you first meet and fall in love, everything is wonderful.

During the stage of starting a family, the dynamics may change. Once you start having children, the focus is not longer on each other—the focus changes. The challenge is to make sure you still find quality time with each other. It can be as simple as a date night or quiet time alone to interact and maintain the intimacy.

Encourage open communication, trust, honesty, and respect. If any of those basic elements are missing from the relationship, problems may arise. If you lose respect for each other, problems will occur.

Some couples have disagreements over money. Lack of money— or the manner that one person manages it—can cause arguments. One spouse may like to live on a budget while the other spends beyond their means. Communication can help address these issues when they occur.

Communication is important to help the other person understand what is important to you. A classic example is the wife withholding sex and the man having no clue why she is mad. She may be upset about something that happened in the past.

If you do not communicate with your mate, how are they going to know why you are upset? Women may hold on to an issue a lot longer than the men. The man may think that the issue has been resolved because they discussed it, but the woman may still be thinking about it. Unhappiness can take shape in many ways.

In every long-term relationship, conflict and disagreement are a part of life. The earlier you establish the ground rules for dealing with the conflict, the better. Sometimes the resolution can be that you agree to disagree. No one is right all of the time—just as no one is perfect. If you believe you are right all the time, conflict will be more difficult to resolve.

You may also want to implement a cooling-off period so both partners can process what the real issue is. This will ensure that you address the root of the problem—and not the symptom. The cooling-off period can also help you avoid saying things that you do not really want to say. Words can hurt—especially if they are coming from a loved one. A great tool for a successful relationship is to never going to bed mad or angry. Work through the issue so it does not linger.

If you are in a long-term relationship, remember to focus on the positive things in the relationship. It is easy to get caught up in the petty things. Ladies, is it a crime if he leaves the toilet seat up? Men, is it a big deal that she does not put the top back on the toothpaste? If that bothers you that much, it is usually an indication that the relationship has bigger problems.

You are with your significant other for a reason. Make mental notes (or written lists) of what you like (or love) about that person. Remind yourself on a regular basis about the positive qualities of the other person. It may be something as simple as he or she makes me laugh or smile. He or she knows me and still loves me.

Since your attention goes where your thoughts flow, keep your attention on all that you love in your partner.

Unconditional love

"If you judge people, you have no time to love them."
—Mother Theresa

Unconditional love is affection with no limits or conditions; complete love. It means to love someone regardless of one's actions or beliefs. It is a concept comparable to true love—a term that is more frequently used to describe love between lovers. By contrast, unconditional love is frequently used to describe love between family members, comrades-in-arms, and other highly committed relationships.

Unconditional love can restore balance, which in turn nurtures our inner peace. I know we have all feel "out of balance" at one time or another. That sensation of feeling "out of sorts" makes us less productive, unhappy, or insecure.

Unconditional love sounds simple, but it is profound. It can be difficult to maintain over long periods of time. Is it possible to love with no limits or conditions? It can seem impossible not to put conditions or expectation on others—especially in a relationship.

People can set expectations when they are dating. Some are of the belief that—after dating for a certain period of time—there is an expectation to marry. Does this mean after one year, two years, or five years, you should get married? Everyone is different and may have different ideas about timing. The timing has to be right for both people.

Unconditional love helps you realize that both people need to be ready to make a serious commitment. If one side is not ready and is pressured into marriage, resentment can build and problems can occur. Some women may feel their biological clock ticking. She may feel pressure to get married quickly. Many men want to feel secure with their career before they make such a serious commitment. This can take a different amount of time for different people, but both people need to be on the same page.

Unconditional love does not mean staying in a bad relationship because you love someone. You should never accept abuse or disrespect from the other person. You can feel love for them and decide you do not want to be in a relationship with them. Loving them does not mean having to live with unhealthy behavior.

You have the right to set limits and know where you are willing to draw the line. If you are in a marriage or relationship and your partner becomes physically abusive, you can leave. This is not a reflection on whether or not you still love him or her. This goes back to respect being one of the foundations of a relationship.

Unconditional love is not a blank check for the other person to treat you badly—no matter the circumstances. Physical or verbal abuse usually represents a bigger issue in the abuser. Maybe it is control or deep-rooted insecurities. Whatever the reason, unconditional love should not stand in the way of getting out of an unhealthy relationship.

A mentor is a trusted friend, counselor, or teacher—usually a more experienced person. Some professions have mentoring programs in which newcomers are paired with more experienced people who advise them and serve as examples as they advance in that profession. Schools sometimes offer mentoring programs to new students—or students with difficulties. The purpose is to help guide and educate. A good mentor has a positive impact on their mentee.

Being a mentor can apply to relationships. This idea is rarely talked about, but it has the perfect application for relationships. If mentors are used to help guide individual behavior, why should that not apply to relationships? Find couples that can share their life lessons with you.

Take a few minutes to think about couples that you know in healthy relationships. Identify a couple with the qualities you would like to have in your healthy relationship. For some, this could be parents or friends. This is not to be confused with a perfect relationship. Remember that the perfect relationship—just like the perfect person—does not exist. Perfection is subjective—it is all about what is perfect for *us*.

Once you have identified your ideal couple, make a list of what you like about their relationship. For example, you may like the fact that they allow each other to be independent while working together as a team.

Take action just like any other mentorship situation:

- Meet with them.
- Listen to them.
- Ask questions.

If more people did this, we could have longer relationships.

If you have the opportunity, it is helpful to go to couple's workshop or retreats. Work at being a couple. The work is not over once you get married—maintaining a healthy relationship is a continuous process.

Couple's counseling can also be very beneficial. It is best not to use counseling as a last resort because waiting too long often leads to attending when the relationship is severely damaged. Coming together as a married couple is a transition for both people and both will need to make adjustments and compromises.

Sex versus Love: Is it Physical or Emotional?

"Passion is the quickest to develop and the
quickest to fade. Intimacy develops more slowly,
and commitment more gradually still."
—Robert Stemberg

How do we know the difference between emotional relationships and physical pleasure? Men and women may have different perspectives on this issue. Some of these perspectives are influenced by religion or culture. In the United States, we are much more geared toward individual satisfaction and personal pleasure. Many of us have bought into a romantic idea of love that can fade over time. If we believe that love is only physical, we many enter a relationship that is not sustainable because there is not enough in common once the initial excitement diminishes.

Generally speaking, when men and women have different thoughts and emotional attachments regarding sex, it stems from our first experience with physical pleasure. Men for the most part have the ability to remove emotional attachment from sex. Their sex drives are much more primal than women's are. As boys, their first sexual experience may not even involve another person. They may have first been stimulated by a magazine or movie. Prostitution is another example of how men can have intercourse without emotional attachment.

On the other hand, most girls have their first sexual experience with someone they really care about—maybe even their first love. Therefore, sex usually with comes with an emotional attachment. There are always exceptions to every rule; more women are removing their emotions from their physical experiences. This is not to say that one is better than the other, but there are differences between the genders and understanding the differences helps to give us perspective.

What we need to understand when it comes to relationships is that sex in and of itself does not make a relationship. If you base a relationship only on sex, it does not usually last. If you want to find or maintain a sane relationship, you need to have more than the physical part in the relationship.

There is a difference between sex and intimacy. Intimacy can include sex, but it is usually a stronger connection. It is an emotional connection with the physical contact.

"Love doesn't make the world go round. Love is what makes the ride worthwhile."
—Franklin P. Jones

"You and I are essentially infinite choice-makers. In every moment of our existence, we are in that field of all possibilities where we have access to an infinity of choices."

—Deepak Chopra

Chapter 6:

Be Empowered by Choices

If we have choices in other areas of our lives, why should relationships be any different? As established in earlier chapters, there are many reasons why people find it difficult to understand that they have choices when it concerns their relationships. Some continue in unhealthy relationships as if they have no say in the matter. People stay in bad relationships for many reasons—most of them for the wrong reason. Fear can be a powerful driver. Maybe they are afraid of being alone or they are afraid of uncertainty. They stay in a relationship because they are afraid of the unknown. *At least I know what to expect in this relationship—even if it is not good for me.*

Another influence can be if they are afraid of hurting the other person's feelings. Telling them that I do not want to be their friend may affect them. What if he or she cannot handle the rejection and does something bad? We cannot take responsibility for other people—we can only be responsible for our own actions.

Insecurity can fill your head with thoughts like these:

- No one is going to want me.
- I am not worthy of being happy.

- If I let this one go, I will never be able to find another person.
- If I let go of this relationship, I will never find someone else.
- I know this relationship is dysfunctional—but it is better than nothing.

The list can go on and on. If you have any of those thoughts, you have the power to introduce new positive thoughts. Rewire you brain with positive thoughts that support the fact that you deserve a sane relationship.

One of the best foundations for a sane relationship is to love yourself enough to know you deserve a healthy relationship. Don't we owe it to ourselves to have healthy relationships? Don't we deserve to be happy? Yes, we do.

Everyone deserves to be happy and we have the choice and power to make it happen. Cleansing negative, unhealthy relationships can give us a sense of personal freedom and newfound power.

Spring Cleaning; both partners have choices; a relationship has to be right for both people.

A relationship, love interest, or friendship has to work for both people. Both sides have to feel as if they are getting something out of it—and putting something into it.

Some people try to force things to work because they like someone. If the feeling is not mutual, it will not work—and may not be a healthy relationship. Only you can decide when to let go of an unhealthy relationship. Friends may try to influence your decision—and some might think you are being selfish. Your life is yours to live—make the choices that make you happy.

Revisit your relationship inventory. If there are any relationships that are toxic in your life, this is the time to let them go. Decide if you want to continue participating in them. If you do not, you have the power to stop participating. You can't change the other person—but you can change whether or not you participate in a relationship with them. For most people, the first step is giving yc permission to let go.

Use release work to release these unhealthy relationships from your life. I know it is easier said than done—and it may take some time to let them go. Letting go may not be forever; if the other person or the dynamics change, you may want to bring that relationship back into your life at a later date.

One Size Does Not Fit All

> "Everything that irritates us about others can lead us
> to an understanding of ourselves." —Carl Jung

The good news about humans is we are all different since no two people are alike, it makes life more interesting. The differences can be many: gender, race, religion, and class, etc. The bad news is that we are all different! The good news remains good news if we are able to accept the differences we all have and do not put our expectations upon others. An expectation that everyone should be just like us or that our way is better.

In The book, *Men are from Mars, Women are from Venus,* Dr. John Gray focuses on the fact that men and women think differently. The more we understand that everyone is different, the better our relationships are. One thing that has worked for me is having many male friends from different backgrounds. Having male friends helps me get a different perspective on my relationships—a perspective that my girlfriends cannot provide. Getting insight from the opposite sex gives me deeper understanding and a greater appreciation for men.

Having friends from different backgrounds allows me to learn about different cultures and customs. It is a big world with lots of different people.

As a result of the differences, no two relationships will be the same. The dynamics of each relationship will be different. Take each lationship on its own merits and understand that one size does not fit all.

Living in the moment can help you appreciate the relationship that is in front of you at the present time.

"The secret of health for both mind and body is not to mourn for the past, not to worry about the future, or not to anticipate troubles, but to live in the present moment wisely and earnestly."

—Buddha

"Life is like a game of cards. The hand
that is dealt you represents determinism:
the way you play it is free will."
—Jawaharlal Nehru

Chapter 7:

Families and Friendships

Family can be one of the most rewarding types of relationship in your life. The unconditional love between a parent and a child cannot be compared to anything else. For most of us, we start our life with family and end our life with family. Many of us have heard that family is all we have. Many of these relationships are at the core of our life and last our entire lifetimes.

Siblings can also be a great support in our lives. We grow up together and share many of the same experiences in our life. Most memories created when we are young involve our siblings and other family members, whether it is immediate or extended family. We can learn so much from our elders. Grandparents give us a historical perspective of our life. Our extended family can also be a great form of comfort. Our aunts, uncles, and cousins can impact our lives.

For some, families can be a challenge. In many families, individual members take on different roles. One may become the nurturer; another (usually the youngest) may take on the baby role and be spoiled. Getting stuck in a role that we are not happy with can become a problem later in life and affect other relationships.

Making choices about our roles in our family is very important for our relationships inside and outside of our families. We can choose whom we marry, but we do not choose our parents, siblings, or extended family.

In the 1970s, the term dysfunctional family was coined. I am not sure I have met anyone who has told me they had a completely functional family—we all have our challenges to experience. Some people compare themselves to the families on television and depending on when you grew up it could be: Ozzie & Harriet, Happy Days, Brady Bunch, Cosby Show or today the George Lopez show. Television shows reflect some of the social issues of the time, but did they really reflect a real family?

Each family has issues or secrets. The level of interaction within each family can be different. In today's complicated world, families can be separated by distance for any number of reasons. Some families communicate every day while others may only connect on holidays.

The ability to resolve issues can also vary by family. Some family members want to discuss the issues while others want to live in denial.

We choose our friends but are born into our family.

Family Inventory

Just as we have done in previous chapters, it is time to make another list. This list should be exclusive to family members. Some of these may have already been included in your first inventory, but it is all right to include them again. This time, really focus on the dynamics of each relationship.

Find a quiet time, clear your mind, and make the list. Once you have listed everyone, go back to each name and think about the person for a few minutes. Let the thoughts and feelings flow. Is there a positive or negative reaction? In some cases, it might be both. Start with the positive thoughts about each person.

- Do you deeply love them?
- Do you admire and respect them?
- Are you grateful for all of the things they have taught you?
- Are you appreciative for their support and unconditional love?
- Do you have a favorite positive memory with them?

Savor any positive energy. Do the same thing for each person and see if there are any uncomfortable emotions that arise (anger, resentment, dislike, or guilt). Use the release exercise to release any negative emotions toward each person. Those thoughts are usually only in your mind.

Release clears our mind of negative thoughts and memories that hold us back from healthy relationships with our family members.

When it comes to having sane relationships with family members, there is no simple answer because no two families are alike. Each family has different dynamics and their own set of experiences that have shaped them as a family unit.

As adults, one of our most powerful tools when relating to family is forgiveness. Whatever has happened can be worked through with forgiveness. No one has the power to change the past, but we have the power to change how we feel about the past and keep it in the past.

> "When you hold resentment toward another, you are
> bound to that person or condition by an emotional
> link that is stronger than steel. Forgiveness is the
> only way to dissolve that link and get free."
> —Catherine Ponder

Many people blame family members and play a victim role. Some people will claim that they are the way they are because their mother, father, or sibling did something to them. There comes a point when we need to accept responsibility for our own actions. When you are an adult, you are able to make choices.

You make your choices—not your parents. We all have had unpleasant experiences, but if we hang onto the past, we will not be able to fully live in the present. Those resentments are probably only hurting you. The other person has their own issues and your issues are probably not at the forefront of their personal agenda. Most likely, that occurrence has long been forgotten.

I think everyone in life has some memory or experience that they hang on to. Since we are all different the same experience can have a different effect. A parent says to their kids, you are not good enough and will never be good enough. The first child may be devastated by the comment, which has lingering effects of never feeling good enough. The next child may use that as motivation and makes an effort to prove the parent wrong and becomes an over achiever. We are all different and have different reactions to the same experience.

There are also in some situations, for self-preservation, we bury extremely negative memories. The tricky thing is that you never know how they will show up later in your life. Those negative memories may cause negative emotions such as anger or resentment. Working toward forgiveness or acceptance helps us let go of the negative emotions toward family members—as well as other people in our life.

Most of us have something from childhood that we need to let go of—and the experiences can be endless. Maybe you feel that your parents were never there for you because they were always working. Maybe you felt that they didn't care about you, but they were just working hard to provide for the family. Maybe you are mad at one parent because your parents divorced. As you look back, you may have a different perspective and understand that it may have been for the better. All relationships begin with yourself and how you react to others is a conscious choice.

What about people who do not have family in their life? Their family members may have passed away or they have been separated by distance or circumstance.

I have a biological family and a "chosen" family. The chosen family are people whom I have selected to be in my life in a way that a family would interact. Healthy friendships can play the role of family members. One is not better that the other—they are just different.

Friends

"My best friend is the one who brings out the best in me."
—Henry Ford

According to Wikipedia, friendship is a cooperative and supportive relationship between two or more people. In this sense, the term connotes a relationship that involves mutual knowledge, esteem, affection, respect, and a degree of rendering service to friends in times of need or crisis. Friends can provide love, support, an ear to listen, and guidance; you can also provide those things for them.

I have a lot of acquaintances, but my friends are people that I have made a choice to have in my life. I have had many of my friends for many years. They are the people who have traveled with me on my journey of life.

Make sure you are a good friend to others. Do not expect something that you are not willing to give yourself. I strive to have friendships that are mutually beneficial. I have also had to make some tough decisions about friendships, and I've let some go if they were filled with drama, toxicity, or negativity.

If you are looking for new friends, search for friends with whom you have something in common. Start with your favorite hobbies and interests. You can make friends at school, work, or in activities involving sports. Doing volunteer work is also a great way to meet new people.

Many people are connecting through social networking. Facebook, MySpace, and Twitter have connected people all over the world. There are more than 308 million people in the United

States and more than 6.8 billion people in the world. If you want to make new friends, you can find them. You just need to be open to finding the right people.

> "The glory of friendship is not the outstretched hand,
> nor the kindly smile, nor the joy of companionship;
> it is the spiritual inspiration that comes to one
> when they discover that someone else believes
> in them and is willing to trust them."
> —Ralph Waldo Emerson

Defining Effective Friendships

Ask yourself what type of friend you want to be. List the qualities that you can bring to a friendship. Make another list of what is important to you about a friendship (loyalty, trustworthiness, or confidentially). Ideally, the two lists are similar.

Set an intention to be the best friend you can be and you will attract that type of friend to your life. Being open when you make new friends is important. One lesson I have learned is that we should not allow other people's opinions or thoughts to influence our ideas about an individual if we do not know them.

In our society, it is easy to be influenced by others without knowing the person. Look at the way the media portrays celebrities, athletes, and political figures. We get so much information about their life that we feel as if we know them—even though we have never met them. We form opinions about them based on the information we have heard, read, or seen on television. The information we have received about that person may not even been true or might have been taken out of context. Our opinion of that person is based on filtered information. As we develop as individuals, we realize that we should base our relationships on the interaction we have with the person—and not by other opinions of that person.

With social media, anybody can say anything about anyone. We all have heard stories of teens bullying each other on Facebook

or MySpace. The extreme example is the mother of one of the te**~~~**
bullying a young girl who later committed suicide. Once the fac**~~~**
came out, everyone realized that the statements about the young girl
were totally fabricated.

The opposite of that is basing your opinion of someone on
your past experiences—completely unrelated to them. Don't let
any relationship be clouded by a relationship with another person
or preconceived thoughts or judgments. Have you ever been in a
situation where you were meeting someone for the first time and they
reminded you of someone you already knew? Were your opinions
or reactions to the new person influenced by the person you already
knew? Always begin new relationships with a fresh start.

Expectations can sometimes interfere with friendships. You may
have expectations in your mind of how a friend should behave. You
may think your friend should call you every day or see you a certain
number of times per week. If the other person does not meet those
expectations, you may become disappointed. Each friendship or
relationship is different; some people talk everyday and some talk
occasionally. Instead of having expectations and then becoming
disappointed, let the other person know what is important to you.

Friendships usually last if there is unconditional caring and both
understand that if either one really needed something; the other
would be there for them.

Just keep in mind that relationships are dynamic, situations can
change and people can change. Friendships are dynamic and you
need to accept responsibility for your side of the fence.

"The only reward of virtue is virtue: the only
way to have a friend is to be a friend."
—Ralph Waldo Emerson

"We make a living by what we get, but
we make a life by what we give."

—Winston Churchill

Chapter 8:

Relationships in the Work World

Work and Career

We now spend a great majority of our adult life at work. When you stop and think about it, there are only twenty-four hours in a day. The average person gets about eight hours of sleep, which leaves you with sixteen waking hours. Most people work at least eight hours per day during the week, so half of your waking hours is spent at work. This does not take into consideration your commute. More people are spending a considerable amount of time either driving to work or taking public transportation. The bottom line is that our careers take up a big part of our lives.

Sometimes we choose to interact with people from our jobs outside of the work environment, and sometimes we choose to keep it separate. Many people choose not to mix business with pleasure. Even if you choose not to socialize with people outside of work, you still spend a good portion of your waking hours interacting with people from your work environment.

Most people spend their lunchtime and coffee breaks with their colleagues. The work environment can foster preconceived opinions coworkers and colleagues. We may have heard things from others and developed judgments before getting to know a person. Make sure you base your relationship on your interactions with that person—not what you may have heard.

In large companies, there will be toxic people and those that thrive on drama and gossip. Most of us have experienced people who thrive on gossip and drama. Their adrenaline gets going. In a bizarre way, they seem to enjoy the drama and don't know how to act if things are calm. They become very judgmental and when a coworker is having challenges, the drama addict uses it as an excuse to put them down. When this happens, I believe they are acting from a place of insecurity.

Think about the last time you heard a coworker making fun of another person. It was as if they were getting joy from someone else's misery. Do not get caught up in judging or criticizing them. When someone else is having a difficult time, we should try to be of service, be there to listen, or stay out of it unless we are asked.

Inventory of Work Relationships

Now is the time to take a look at whom you are interacting with at work. In a work environment, we usually have little say over *whom* we interact with. However, we still have power over *how* we interact with them. You have control over your actions—not theirs.

Take a few moments to make your list. List your boss and coworkers. If you are the boss, list your team.

- Is my interaction with my coworkers' professional?
- Do I act with integrity?
- How effective is my communication?
- Am I holding any resentment toward this person?
- Do I have a healthy relationship with this person?

Once you have made the list, sit down and analyze it. As previously discussed, you may not have choices about the people around you at work, but if you have any resentments or negative feelings about anyone on your list, let them go for your own well being. Because that resentment will fester over time and can cause you more problems than it will for the other person.

Ask yourself if there is any way to improve your relationship with the person. In the workplace, one of the most important factors in healthy relationships is communication. Effective communication is a powerful tool—use it. Release the coworker who enjoys the drama or water cooler gossip. It is not a relationship you may want to foster.

By human nature, we are curious about each other; almost everyone engages in conversations about other people. However, there is a difference between sharing information about someone and spreading judgments about him or her. If someone in your workplace gets a promotion, it would be understandable to share that information with a coworker. Some people might add their individual opinion when discussing the promotion—and making it their perception instead of factual.

For example, Mary in the office shares that Nicole got a promotion, but then she says, "I bet she got the promotion because she was brown-nosing the boss." The second part of that is Mary's opinion and perception.

Gossip and judgments are not based on gender. Men in work environments can engage in spreading negative opinions just as much as women can.

You may work with drama queens, but it does not mean you have to engage in the negativity. Rise above the drama and stay focused on work.

If you are on the receiving end of the rumors and gossip, you need to have thick skin and ignore them. Do not engage in it. Once you start defending yourself, you are giving power to the person that thrives on drama.

> "When you judge another, you do not
> define them, you define yourself."
> —Wayne Dyer

The decision to have relationships with the people you work with is a very individual decision and can be influenced by many factors. Remember to make good decisions for you.

Relationships can also be determined—and changed—by the roles people have in the workplace. For example, John was your coworker for several years and you had a great relationship with him. When John gets a promotion and becomes your boss, the dynamics in your relationship change because the roles are different. When he was your coworker, you would joke around and share information about things outside of work. You may have experienced external office socializing or happy hours. Now that he is your boss, the interaction is less frequent and he appears very distant. His new role as boss can impact how he interacts with you. Don't take these changes personally; he may be getting used to his new role as an authority figure.

> "Don't take anything personally. Nothing others
> do is because of you. What others say and do is a
> projection of their own reality, their own dream. When
> you are immune to the opinions and actions of others,
> you won't be the victim of needless suffering."
> —Don Miguel Ruiz

What about dating in the workplace? I know many people who have met their spouses at work; after all, we spend so much of our waking hours at work. While it may work, here are a few words of caution: make sure you are not involved with someone whom you supervise or who supervises you. Most companies prohibit that. Not only is it banned by most companies, sexual harassment laws apply in some states. If you are dating your boss and others feel you are getting special treatment because of it, your coworkers can file sexual harassment charges against him or her.

The other pitfall of dating someone you work with is if it does not work out, you are going to see that person on a regular basis. This could be awkward—and an open invitation for your coworkers to engage in gossip about you. Dating someone at work depends on a lot of factors—do what is right for you.

The other situation that does not usually have a happy ending is dating a married coworker or dating someone at work when you are married. This happens many times and inevitably people get hurt. Coworkers in these unhealthy relationships fool themselves into thinking that no one knows about it. However, usually the entire workplace knows what is going on and it affects the office environment.

Ask yourself if the relationship is worth losing your job if people find out. Several years ago, a colleague who had worked for the same company for most of his career, was a few years away from retirement. He was smart, respected, and had worked his way up the ranks over the years. He was married and was having an affair with a much younger employee who was also married. When the affair came out, his wife gave him an ultimatum to retire or divorce. When he took an early retirement and left the job with an air of shame around him, there was no retirement party and no fanfare after more than three decades of hard work. The other relationship ended in divorce, which hurt her husband and her son. Consider the consequences of your actions.

In some circumstances, socializing or dating colleagues may be the only option you feel you have. For example, you may be new to a city and not have any friends or family. The coworkers are your only relationships. That may suit your needs for short periods of time, but it is important to develop additional friendships outside of your work environment in the long run. You can meet people volunteering at community organizations, church, through your children's school, or in groups where you have similar hobbies or interests. Many people use the Internet to connect on social networking sites. The advancement of technology has made the world smaller. You can make friends and meet people all over the world. Technology has connected us to many people but remember that nothing can replace the experience of spending time together or talking on the phone. Keep the human touch in your relationships.

In today's changing world, people experience new jobs several times in their careers. It is rare to stay with one company for your entire life. In each new work environment, take the time to evaluate each new situation since no two relationships are exactly the same. Do your work inventories if you are in a new work environment or on an annual basis for those in the same work environment.

"The last of the human freedoms is to choose one's attitude in any given set of circumstances."
—Viktor Frankl

"There are two primary choices in life: to accept conditions as they exist, or accept the responsibility for changing them."
—Denis Waitley

Chapter 9:

Sustainable Relationships

The key to a sustainable relationship is plain and simple: it takes work. If it is worth it, you will want to do the work. Once you establish trust, respect, and communication in a relationship, it can last for long periods of time. A sustainable relationship takes work on both sides. If one side is doing all the work, it can lead to resentment, anger, and unhappiness. Those emotions can come out in unexpected ways and are not conducive to a healthy relationship.

Remain grateful for the people in your life. When you find healthy relationships, nurture them and surround them with a field of gratitude. Express your gratitude—it can be as simple as telling the other person that you love them. Be there for them in their time of need. Listen to them when they need to talk or cry on a shoulder.

Everything that you would want in a friend, give as a friend. Everything you want in a relationship, give in a relationship. Do not fall into the blame game; take time to look in the mirror. Address the issue when it arises, and do not let the problems fester and cause negative emotions.

Doing the Work

Now that you have the necessary skills, it is time to do the work. All relationships require work, including working on yourself. Taking a regular inventory of your happiness and the relationships in your life is important. Periodically, you may find that you need to evaluate your life and release whatever is not working for you. These tools can be used at any point in your life. Retake each inventory whenever you feel out of balance. Retake the SHE test and do the release work to remove any obstacles that are blocking you from your ultimate happiness. Remember that happiness is a choice—and choose happiness every day of your life!

You are the common denominator in all relationships in your life, if you are healthy, whole and complete you have a better chance of having healthy relationships in your life.

Annual Assessment

It helps to reevaluate your life on an annual basis. I find it helpful to do it around my birthday. My birthday is January 5. My annual assessment goes along with setting intentions for the New Year. I do not make New Year's resolutions since we all know that most of us do not keep them past January. I set intentions or goals that keep my energy flowing forward. I recommend you do the following on an annual basis:

- Retake the SHE test. Life is dynamic—maybe things have changed in your life. Maybe there are new things that have arisen that are holding you back from being happy.
- Do the release work to shed the issues that are holding you back from your happiness. Set specific intentions for sane relationships in your life. Take an inventory of the people in your life and liberate yourself from toxic relationships.

- Focus on being grateful for the positive people and the blessings that have been bestowed upon you.
- Keep open and honest communication with those you care most about—including yourself.
- Use the tools you have learned in this book as often as necessary. You are responsible for your happiness. If you are not willing to do the work, who will do it for you? Life is constantly changing and you are continuously evolving.
- Living is a process that continues to unfold until you make your transition. Choose sane relationships. They will help you stay balanced in this crazy world.
- Choose happiness, happiness is a choice. Choose happiness every day of your life
- Do the work and reap the rewards. Read the quotes in this book—or find quotes that inspire you!

"Every time you are tempted to react in the same old way, ask if you want to be a prisoner of the past or a pioneer of the future."
—Deepak Chopra

"Realize deeply that the present moment
is all you ever have. Make the Now
the primary focus of your life."

—Eckhart Tolle

Chapter 10:

Your New Beginning

In this book, I have tried to share my own perception of reality. My perception is based upon my experiences. This is not to say that everything I have said will apply to everyone. Since each of us—and each relationship—is different, those combinations create infinite possibilities when it comes to dynamics in relationships. Find what you feel comfortable with and what resonates with you.

For me, this final chapter is one of the most important because I believe that all relationships start and end with God. When I feel at one with God, I am happiest in my relationships. When I am happy, my side of the relationship is sane.

I would be remiss if I did not mention the most important relationship that one can develop if you want to live a balanced life is the relationship with a higher power. Some people choose to call this power God, but others have different names to describe the creator. The name doesn't matter—the connection does.

All over the world, different names are used for the same thing. My Native American roots have taught me to call this energy Great Sprit. There is a power that is bigger than us all—and, by virtue, we are all connected. Whatever name you choose, it is up to you.

I personally choose to believe in God, but I am open to having everyone use words that feel right to them.

By believing in this higher power and universal laws, we can also see that there are people that are put into our lives for different reasons—some for a specific reason and others for a season. Some people have an intermittent relationship with God and only reach out when they are in need. Some people pray when they are in crisis. But just like any other relationship, it should be there in good times and bad times. We need to have a positive relationship with our creator to keep our relationships sane and balanced.

Having faith can also give us the courage to get rid of relationships that no longer work for us. When we are challenged with bad relationships, we can be gifted the strength to release them.

Listening to that intuition can help us in many aspects of our lives—not just in relationships. Even if we are in denial, our intuition tells us when a relationship is not good. How many times have we told ourselves that something inside told felt wrong? *Why didn't I listen?* Being balanced in harmony with the universe will allow us to receive the messages we need to hear.

Having a solid relationship with a higher being teaches us the elements of a healthy relationship: honesty, respect, and trust.

As you travel your life journey in this crazy world, I hope you find sane relationships filled with love and happiness! The choice is yours. Once you find happiness and feel secure with yourself, you will be surprised how all your relationships are better!

You may find that periodically you need to reevaluate your life and release whatever is not working for you. Take inventory, retake the SHE test, and do the release work to remove your obstacles.

In this crazy world, clutter in our life can sneak up on us. I know that you are capable of finding sane relationships in this crazy world—you just need to do the work to get there.

Daily prayer helps keep me centered and grounded. I would like to share with you a prayer that I wrote:

Great Spirit, creator who I call God.
I humbly stand before you, to praise you.
For you are I…. and….. I am you.
I welcome you into my heart, body & soul.
Great Spirit, God Creator of All

Grant me the wisdom to follow my inner voice,
The strength to stay grounded while I sing my scared song,
Guide me down my chosen path with the courage
to pursue what is available to me.
Great Spirit, God Creator of All

Allow me to receive the infinite possibilities of the universe.
I am appreciative for my lessons yet grateful for the struggles,
I am comforted by the wonderful people you have placed in my life.
Great Spirit, God Creator of All

I honor Mother Earth for the gifts she provides.
The fertile soil provides our daily food & the
gift of water is the essence of life.
Open my heart to the healing of nature.
We are all related and through this I find serenity.
Great Spirit, God Creator of All.

May I never stop being a beneficial presence on this planet.
Work through me to carry the message of
peace and unconditional love.
I am complete having you in my life.
Great Spirit, God, Creator of All

And so it is…Hallelujah ………..Amen

Write your own prayer that you can use in your life. Use whatever words or thoughts you need in your life.

I have included many of my favorite quotes. These quotes help me in my life so find quotes that resonates with you. We can all learn from each other.

I am grateful that you have taken the time to hear my perspective on sane relationships. As I have stated, I do not have all the answers; however, if there is anything in this book that can help to improve your life, I am glad to have shared my lessons.

I wish you joy, love, peace, and happiness—but, most of all, I hope you find the sane relationships that you deserve.

Peace and blessings,
Cynthia M. Ruiz

CPSIA information can be obtained at www.ICGtesting.com
Printed in the USA
LVOW041500050512

280428LV00001B/4/P